AF374808

Mom, You Did It!
Copyright © 2023 Tameka Mitchell
All rights reserved. No part of this book may be reproduced in any form,
stored in any retrieval system, or transmitted in any form by any means
electronic, mechanical, photocopy, recording, or otherwise-without prior
written permission of the author or publisher.

ISBN 979-8-9865130-3-4

Book design by Praise Z. Saflor

First Edition, 2023

Published in the United States by
Maternity Motivation Publishing, LLC

maternitymotivation.com

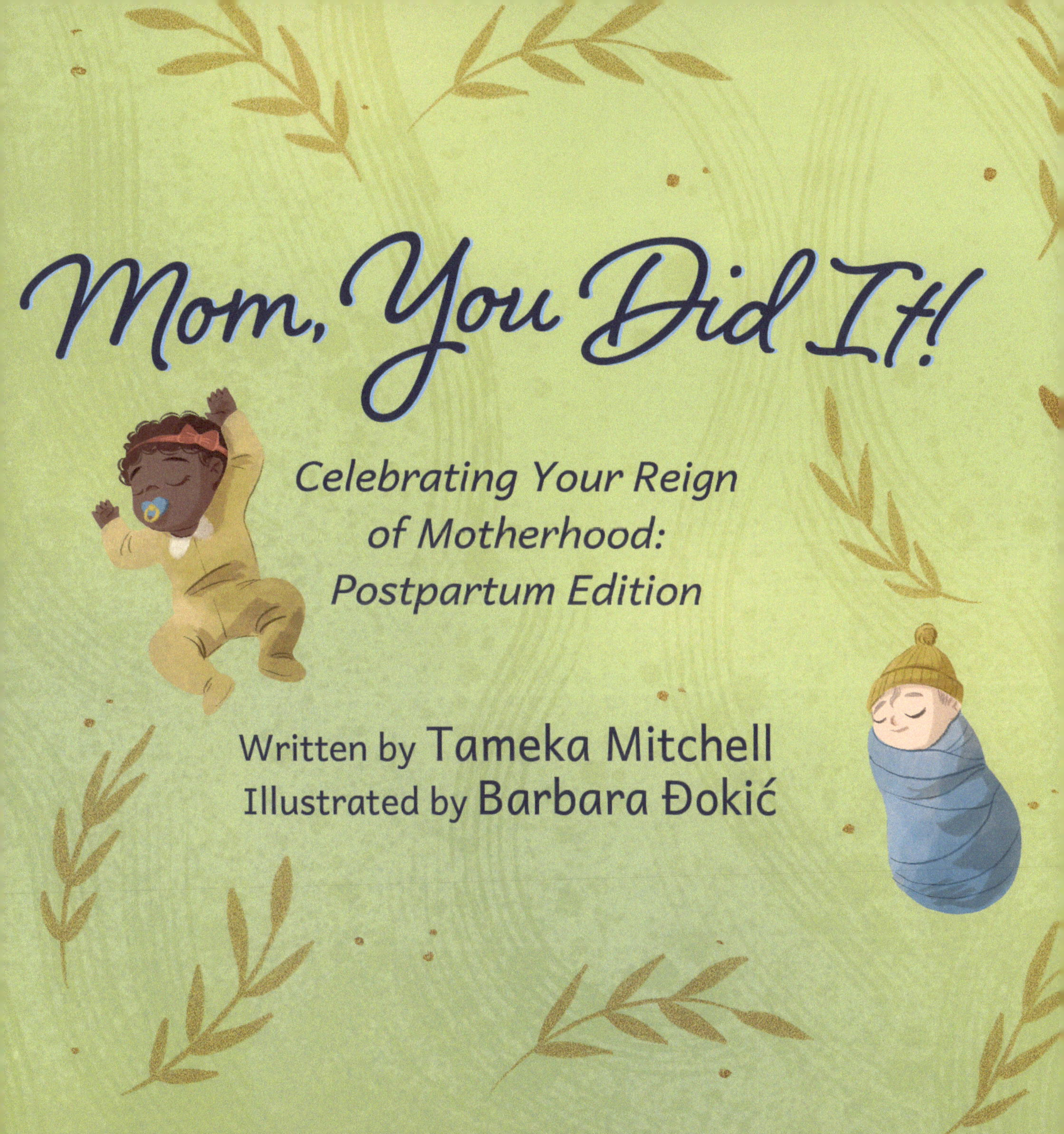

Mom, You Did It!

Celebrating Your Reign
of Motherhood:
Postpartum Edition

Written by **Tameka Mitchell**
Illustrated by **Barbara Đokić**

Mom, You Did It!

Girl, we love you so much! You have prepared for this exciting new arrival and your little one has made their debut.

For some, the pregnancy was tough and you are simply exhausted.

Your family is in awe of your strength: today, tomorrow, and for years to come.

Lovingly, it's game time!

In this new chapter, you will see that the world is an amazing place through the eyes of your child.

You will learn so much about yourself and others. My friend, don't be afraid to ask for help.

Mom, make sure you are resting
to regain your strength.

There are plenty of moments for hugs
and kisses—however you're a champion
who needs to pace yourself.

If you are not feeling well, let the nurses know.
Your team is ready and will be right by your side.

Grace
the Lactation Nurse

We are proud of you!
Tell us how you are feeling.

We can't wait to hear how you bond with your baby, because it's very special.

Yet bonding looks different from one mother to the next.

Moms do not have all the answers,
just make sure you do your best.

Remember, this is new for everyone and we all need to practice patience and grace.

The nurses have given good advice on how to take care of yourself.

HOSPITAL

It's time to go home.

Take it one step at a time. You are still recovering.

There is no such thing as a perfect day.

Bedtime Routine

Have
Faith
Family
Loves
You
Trust your
BIG
Ideas

How can I better support her?
We are a team!
What are we doing? Motherhood concierge

You are supported!

Mother Empowerment Declaration:

Look in the mirror and greet yourself by name.
Say the following:

I do not know the last time I told you
"I love you" but now is the moment.

You are capable.

You are more aware of your actions.

And do not overextend yourself because your
health is precious.

Remember to take deep breaths (practice).

Listen, learn, and do your best.

I believe in YOU!

Moms,
Prioritize your mental, physical,
and emotional health just as closely
as baby's check-ups.

Educate, engage, and unite
with other moms using local
postpartum resources.

We found them helpful!

Add Tameka Mitchell,
Chief Mom Motivator
to your support team.